Inside SPORT

GOLF

Clive Gifford

First published in 2009 by Wayland

Copyright © Wayland 2009

Wayland
338 Euston Road
London NW1 3BH

Wayland Australia
Level 17/207 Kent Street
Sydney NSW 2000

Commissioning Editor: Jennifer Sanderson
Designer: Robert Walster, Big Blue Design
Illustrator: Ian Thompson
Picture Researcher: Clive Gifford
Proofreader: Katie Dicker

Picture Acknowledgements:
The author and publisher would like to thank the following agencies for allowing these pictures to be reproduced: Cover, 34 Andrew Redington/Getty Images Sport; 3, 27 Stuart Franklin/Getty Images Sport; 5, 19 David Cannon/Getty Images Sport; 6 Hunter Martin/Getty Images Sport; 7 Robyn Beck/AFP; 8 IStock; 9 top IStock; 9 bottom Brian Bahr/Getty Images Sport; 10 David Cannon/Getty Images Sport; 11 Mark Ralston/AFP; 12 Ross Kinnaird/Getty Images Sport; 13 Karen Bleier/AFP; 14 IStock; 15 top IStock; 15 bottom Mizuno Gallery; 16 Kazuhiro Nogi/AFP; 17 Stuart Franklin/Getty Images Sport; 18 Stuart Franklin/Getty Images Sport; 20 Stuart Franklin/Getty Images Sport; 21 Stephen Dunn/Getty Images Sport; 22 David Cannon/Getty Images Sport; 23 Andy Lyons/Getty Images Sport; 24 Chris Condon/US PGA Tour; 25 David Cannon/Getty Images Sport; 26 Robyn Beck/AFP; 28 Stan Honda/AFP; 29 David Cannon/Getty Images Sport; 30 Darren Carroll/Sport's illustrated; 31 Paul Severn/Getty Images Sport; 33 Scott Halleran/Getty Images Sport; 34 Andy Lyons/Getty Images Sport; 35 Timothy A. Clary/AFP; 37 Adrian Dennis/AFP; 38 Fred Vuich/Sports Illustrated; 39 Stan Honda/AFP; 40 Ross Kinnaird/Getty Images Sport 41 Scott Halleran/Getty Images Sport; 42 Brian Morgan/Getty Images Sport; 43 Augusta National/Getty Images Sport; 44 Mizuno Gallery

British Library Cataloguing in Publication Data
 Gifford, Clive
   Golf. - (Inside sport)
   1. Golf - Juvenile literature
   I. Title
   796.3'52

ISBN: 978 0 7502 5709 1

Printed in China

Wayland is a division of Hachette Children's Books,
an Hachette UK company
www.hachette.co.uk

CONTENTS

Introduction 6

The early days 8

Aim of the game .10

Where to play 12

Equipment .14

Rules and officials 16

Caddies and coaches 18

Tactics and techniques 20

On the tee 22

Shot selection 24

Short game 26

Pressure putting 28

Recovery shots 30

The big competitions 32

The Masters 34

The Open Championship 36

The US Open and PGA Championships 38

The Ryder and Solheim Cups 40

Golfing legends 42

Glossary 44

Websites 45

Index 46

INTRODUCTION

Played and watched by millions, golf tests players' technique, fitness and nerve as they use a club to hit a ball around a course in the fewest possible shots.

A Full Course

Some golf courses are made up of nine holes, which players go around twice, but a full course consists of 18 individual holes. Completing these is known as a 'round of golf'. Each hole starts with a tee area from where a player takes his or her first shot (a drive). At the other end, is the green, made of smooth, short grass. The hole itself, which is 10.8 centimetres in diameter and is marked by a 2-metre high flag, is on the green. Between the tee and the green are obstacles, from steep slopes and lakes to sand-filled depressions, called bunkers, and thick grass and heather, known as rough. Many holes also have an area of mowed grass between the tee and the green. This is called the fairway. Every hole on a course is different, and all golfers have their most- and least-favourite holes and courses.

Professional Golf

The top players are wealthy professionals, who are paid to play in tournaments. Tournament golf is played mostly over four full rounds, making 72 holes in total. The golfer who takes the fewest number of

American professional golfer Paula Creamer hits a long drive down the fairway.

shots to complete all 72 holes, is the winner. A major tournament is full of incidents, thrills and spills as some players surge up the leader board while others fall away.

After two rounds, the number of players in a tournament is usually reduced. Players whose scores are low enough to continue are said to have made the cut. As the final round is completed, the tension mounts. A player who has finished his or her round and is in front, is called the clubhouse leader. If two players tie with the same number of shots, a play-off is usually played over a number of extra holes, with the lowest-scoring player victorious. In most forms of tournament golf, there can be only one winner.

Tiger Woods plays out of a bunker during the play-off at the 2008 US Open. Despite a knee injury, he won the tournament.

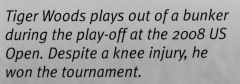

?

Who is...

...Tiger Woods?

The most famous golfer on the planet, Eldrick 'Tiger' Woods started playing at a young age, winning the World Junior championship six times. He has continued to be the sport's most successful player, notching up over 90 tournament wins. Woods has also been the PGA (Professional Golfer's Association) Player of the Year nine times and has hit 18 holes-in-one. Tiger is not only an exciting player, but he is also remarkably consistent. From 1998 to 2005, he made 142 tournament cuts in a row – the next-best golfer at the time was Ernie Els with just 20.

THE EARLY DAYS

Golf has a long and illustrious history with some of its most famous courses and competitions being in place long before some sports had playing rules.

The First Clubs

No one knows where golf was invented. Although *paganica* – an Ancient Roman game using curved clubs, and balls stuffed with feathers – was similar to today's game. Golf as we know it developed in Scotland. A primitive version of the game was so popular in Scotland 450 years ago that it was banned because it was interfering with people practising archery to defend their country! By the eighteenth century, golf in Scotland was organised with clubs and courses in Edinburgh and at the St Andrews course in Fife. In 1754, the club at St Andrews was formed. It later became known as the Royal and Ancient and by the nineteenth century, it was considered the chief rule-maker of the sport. The first major tournament, The Open Championship was held in 1860 and at the same time, the game spread to Europe and North America.

MAD FACT

In 2005, American golfers spent an astonishing US$763 million on new balls.

This is one of golf's most famous buildings – the clubhouse at the Old Course of St Andrews in Scotland.

Early Equipment

Early courses varied greatly in their number of holes. St Andrews originally had 22 holes while an early Edinburgh course had just five. Players would use wooden clubs to hit Featherie balls, which were made from wet goose feathers packed into a leather ball. These balls were hand-made and very expensive. In the 1850s they were replaced with a rubber-like Gutta-Percha ball. Iron clubs were available but rarely used, while steel-shafted clubs were banned in British golf by the Royal and Ancient until 1929 because they were too different from the iron clubs.

An early wooden club and Featherie golf ball. These balls were made of tightly-stitched panels of leather stuffed with boiled goose and chicken feathers. Featheries were used well into the nineteenth century.

Etiquette

Early in golf history, a series of customs and polite ways of acting, known as etiquette, developed. Most of these customs continue today and mean that players have respect for the course and each other. They include staying still and silent when another player takes a shot, shouting 'fore!' to alert other golfers when a wild shot is hit, and waiting for the hole ahead to be clear of golfers before taking a shot. Players are expected to keep their bags or trolleys off the green, to repair any dents that balls pitching (bouncing) on the green have made, and not to step on the line of another golfer's putt. Golfers unsure of the etiquette should always ask more experienced golfers for advice.

Sergio Garcia (left) and Dean Wilson repair pitch marks on a green. A pitch mark is a small dent in the green caused by a ball landing. Repairing them is an example of good golf etiquette.

AIM OF THE GAME

The aim of golf is to hit the ball, in as few shots or strokes as possible, from the tee into the hole. This is a test of players' technique and how accurately they can repeat the swing of their club each time.

Paul Casey swings to make sure the ball avoids the bunker on his left, but lands safely on the green.

Grip and Swing

A player grips the top of the club with both hands and stands with his or her feet apart and knees flexed. To send the ball in the right direction, the player makes sure his or her body, feet and club are aligned. The golfer swings by taking the club head back from behind the ball, cocking (bending) his or her wrists and turning his or her hips and shoulders. The player's body coils at the top of the backswing and then uncoils as the club is brought down on the downswing. The club makes clean contact with the ball and follows through. The golfer's hips turn and finally, after the ball has already flown away, the player's head swivels to point over the shoulder with his or her chest facing the target as the club travels over the other shoulder.

Keeping Score

Players record the number of shots they take to complete a hole on their scorecards, which in tournaments they must sign and present to the officials. Each hole has a par – the number of shots it is thought to take by a good golfer. Taking one shot more than par is called a bogey and two shots more, a double-bogey. To finish a hole in one shot less than par is known as a birdie, two less an eagle, and three an albatross. A hole-in-one is a celebrated achievement. The oldest golfer to achieve this is Elsie McLean in 2007 – she was 102 years old!

Australian Gary Simpson, lines up a putt in front of the scoreboard on the second day of the Volkswagen Masters-China in 2005. He finished the day at 10 under par despite playing the round without a 5 iron, which he broke in practise.

HOLE	PLAYER	+/−PAR	TOTAL
16	SIMPSON		−10
	GOOSEN		−8
17	RUSNAK		−7
17	WARREN		−6
	GRIFF		−6

The two most common scoring systems are stroke play (the total number of strokes taken to complete all the holes) and match play, mainly found in team golf such as the Ryder Cup (see page 40). Match play is based on a hole-per-hole basis – the player who completes the hole in the least number of shots wins the hole. If the players complete the hole in the same number of shots then the hole is said to be halved. The player or pair of players who wins the most holes in the round, wins.

Handicaps

Handicaps enable golfers of different abilities to play against each other. A handicap is the number of shots (usually between 1 and 24 for men and 1 and 36 for women and juniors) that are removed from a player's final score. Handicaps are effectively a head start for a player who is less able and has a higher handicap than a better player. Professional players play off a handicap of zero, known as scratch.

(see page 40)

STAT ATTACK

Lowest Score in PGA Golf

59 - Al Geiberger: 1977 Memphis Classic

59 - Chip Beck: 1991 Las Vegas Invitational

59 - David Duval: 1999 Bob Hope Chrysler Classic

WHERE TO PLAY

There are more than 33,000 golf courses around the world and about half of those are in the United States. Added to this are thousands of shorter pitch-and-putt courses, driving ranges, practise holes and putting greens.

Practise Places

There are many aids to help players practise their golf. Out on open land, air balls can be driven hard but they do not travel far because they have holes in their surface to slow them down. Beginners and more experienced players often find driving ranges helpful. These consist of a series of bays from which golfers can hit balls onto a wide communal fairway, which is usually marked with targets and distance markers. At a tournament golf course, there are plenty of practise facilities, too, including a driving range, putting green and practise holes. Golf nets are tubular metal frames covered in mesh or netting, which allow players to hit the ball as hard they wish in a small space because the ball is caught in the net.

The Coober Pedy golf course in Australia has no grass. Players carry a piece of artificial turf with them to place the ball on before it is hit. The greens are covered in oil to make the sand stick together and not blow away.

green

rough

rough

green

fairway

bunker

An aerial view of part of the scenic Pinnacle Point golf course in South Africa.

Course Design

Golf holes vary in length. The shortest are not much more than 109.3 yards (100 metres) while par 5 holes can be longer than 546.8 yards (500 metres). The length of a hole tends to guide its par score. Most golf courses also rate their holes in degrees of difficulty with one being the toughest hole to complete in par and 18, the easiest. Courses are built to present challenges to golfers and no two holes are the same. Designers use hazards, such as rough, trees and water features, to divide the holes. Some holes are 'doglegs' with the hole angled like a bent arm so that golfers cannot see the green from the tee.

MAD FACT

Scotsman Thomas Bendelow arrived in New York in 1892. By the time of his death in 1936, he had designed over 800 golf courses in Canada and the United States.

Greenkeepers closely mow the grass around the fringes of the 11th green at Oakland Hills before the start of the 2008 PGA Championship. Top courses take thousands of hours of work to prepare before an important tournament.

Course Preparation

Courses are kept in excellent condition by the ground staff or greenkeepers. Dozens of staff are involved in the run-up to a major tournament. All aspects of preparation, from how closely the greens are mowed (this affects their speed) to the position of the teeing area and holes on the green, are decided by the course or tournament committee. Whether at a tournament or on a local course, golfers are expected to do their bit to look after the course. This includes raking bunkers smooth after playing a shot and replacing the piece of turf, called a divot, that becomes loose when a shot on the fairway is hit.

EQUIPMENT

In competition golf, players are allowed up to 14 clubs in their bags. These consist of a putter for use on the greens, one or more wedges for short shots, a series of irons and a small number of woods.

Golf Clubs

A club features a rubber or leather grip, a shaft made of steel, carbon-fibre or a metal alloy, and the head. Woods are so called because originally they were made from wood, but now titanium and light, but strong metal alloys are used to make the head. Woods are mostly used when driving because they can send the ball long distances. However, some players like to use a fairway wood, such as a 3-wood or 4-wood, off the fairway.

MAD /// FACT

In 2008, UK company Geotate announced plans to place a chip inside golf balls. The chip could track the ball's speed, distance and precise location on the golf course using satellite technology.

The face of all clubs, except the putter, is angled back to provide loft (height). The greater the angle of the club face, the higher in the air and less distance forward the ball will travel. Sand and pitching wedges have the most loft. They are used for close-range shots and for getting out of hazards, such as bunkers. Other irons are numbered, usually from 1–9. The lower the number, the lower the amount of loft and the longer the shaft. Some players may use a 1, 2, 3 or 4 iron, typically known as long irons, when driving off the tee.

The heads of a long iron (right), a medium iron and a wedge show how the shorter the iron, the greater the angle or loft of the club. More loft sends a ball up higher but over a shorter forward distance.

Golf Balls

Supercomputers and high-tech science go into the design of modern golf balls. Most are made of an inner core, a wound mid-section and a tough protective covering. The outer surface is covered in hundreds of small dimples. These help to create lift, reduce drag and allow the ball to travel further than if it was smooth. All balls have to be at least 42.67 millimetres in diameter and must weigh less than 45.93 grams.

A golfer tees up his ball before making a drive. A tee is a peg used to raise the ball off the ground and help the golfer make cleaner contact with the ball.

MAD /// /// FACT

In 1985, a World One-Club Championship was held. It was won by Thad Daber who used a 6 iron for every shot to complete his round in 73 shots.

Clothing and Kit

In addition to clubs and balls, golfers store a range of other items in their bags. They use towels and brushes to clean and dry the faces and grips of their clubs, tees to raise the ball when driving from the teeing area and pitch repairers to repair the green after a ball has landed. Golfers wear spiked shoes that provide grip but do not damage the course. Most professional golfers wear clothing sponsored by sportswear companies. Some golfers are known for a particular way of dressing. For example, Ian Poulter is renowned for dressing flamboyantly, while Gary Player was known as 'the Black Knight' for wearing all black.

Ignacio Garrido poses with his golf bag and clubs. Professional golfers work closely with their club manufacturers on the design and production of their ideal tournament clubs.

RULES AND OFFICIALS

Golf relies on players being honest and admitting when they have made a mistake. Mistakes often result in one or more penalty shots added to a player's score. At tournaments, officials help to uphold the rules and ensure that fair play occurs.

The Ball's Lie

Once all the players in a group have teed off, they walk to find their balls. The golfer furthest from the flag takes the next shot. Where the ball comes to rest after a shot is known as its lie. One of golf's core rules is that the ball is played as it lies. This means that if it has run into a dip in the ground or up against a bush, it has to be played from that position. If a player decides that he or she really cannot play the ball, a stroke is added to the player's total and he or she can then drop the ball two club lengths away from its original position, but not nearer the hole. However, there are exceptions to this rule: if the ball lands in an area of ground under repair or beside a young tree or on some paths, a player can have a free drop and move the ball a club length away, but not nearer the hole, without adding shots to his or her score.

David Duval weighs up his options to get his ball out of rough during a tournament in Japan.

Penalty Strokes

Should a rule be broken, penalty strokes can be added to a golfer's score. For example, players are not allowed to move the ball on the way to the green – if they do, a penalty stroke is added. Golfers can pick up the ball on the green to clean it or to remove it from the path of another golfer's putt, but only if they mark its position beforehand. When in a bunker, golfers are not allowed to touch the sand with their club before making the shot, otherwise they have to add two shots to their score.

MAD //// //// FACT

In Uganda, the golfers at the Jinga golf club are permitted a free drop if their ball lands in a hippopotamus's footprint. They must also stop playing and give way to the elephants that occasionally roam the course.

A referee joins Mike Weir and Jarmo Sandelin on the 12th green at the Hong Kong Open tournament. Referees offer on-the-spot rulings on tricky issues during a competition.

Marshals and Referees

At tournaments, marshals help to keep the crowd in check and the competition running smoothly. Some carry portable scoreboards, while others raise signs to insist on silence when a shot is played. Referees go from hole to hole to make rulings on various matters, such as whether or not a player can have a free drop. In tournaments, players mark each other's scorecards but it is up to each golfer to check the scorecard and sign it before handing it in. In 2000, Padraig Harrington forgot to sign his scorecard. Despite him leading the tournament, he was disqualified.

CADDIES AND COACHES

Professional golfers have a small team around them. They may have a business manager or agent who handles appearances and sponsorship deals, as well as someone who arranges all their travel. Vital to any player's performance are two people – the player's caddie and coach.

Fanny Sunesson advises Henrik Stenson on the yardage to various hazards on a hole. She has caddied for Nick Faldo, Sergio Garcia and Martin Kaymer.

Top Caddies

A professional golf caddie is far more than someone who carries a golfer's bag of clubs. Caddies have an in-depth understanding of golf and especially their golfer, knowing how to coax or encourage them and when to keep quiet. Top caddies are expected to pass on crucial information such as wind direction, course conditions and club selection to their player.

Caddies are usually paid a salary and a percentage of the player's winnings – seven to ten per cent is typical. Many caddies work for short periods with a range of golfers. For example, Fanny Sunesson has caddied for Nick Faldo, Michelle Wie, Mark Hensby and Henrik Stenson. Some golfers, however, stick with the same caddie for many years. Steve Williams has been Tiger Woods' caddie since 1999, which is believed to have made him a multi-millionaire.

Getting the Yardage

In most countries, holes and shots are measured in yards, but in some, they are measured in metres. A hole's yardage is the distance from the tee to the hole. Caddies build up a detailed yardage chart of parts of a golf course. These charts give the distances from the tee (and other locations) to various points on the hole – from the flag and front of the green to notable hazards. Golfers know the typical distance they can hit with each club. By looking at the yardage chart they aim to match the club to the shot to be played.

MAD FACT

During a 1979 tournament, Curtis Strange had to finish his round with just four clubs after his caddie, Mark Freiburg, dropped the others into a water hazard.

Golf Coaches

As a beginner, the best way to learn to play golf is to have lessons from a professional coach or teacher. However, lessons and coaching can be useful throughout a golfer's career because even the top players flock to golf coaches, such as Butch Harmon and David Leadbetter, for advice. Harmon coached Tiger Woods early in his career and has also coached Greg Norman, Davis Love III and Adam Scott, while Leadbetter has given advice and swing tips to several golfers including Nick Faldo, Ernie Els, Nick Price and Michelle Wie.

Coach David Leadbetter watches Trevor Immelman in practise at a driving range in Florida. A player may employ a coach at a tournament for advice on tweaking their swing between rounds.

TACTICS AND TECHNIQUES

Professional golfers work exceptionally hard at their game so that they can enter a tournament in the best possible shape. Ahead of them are 72 holes of competition that will place great strains on their technique, mental strength and decision making.

MAD //// //// FACT

In 2009, the Dubai World Championship will be the world's richest tournament with prize money of US$10 million.

Grooving their Game

Top golfers work on their swing so that it is second nature to them. They need to be able to repeat it again and again, especially under the great pressure they face in tournaments. To be a good golfer, the full swing, which is used for most of their drives and fairway shots, needs to remain accurate and consistent across all the clubs in a golfer's bag. Golfers spend much time practising shots, such as short chips onto the green and specialist shots out of rough and bunkers, as well as the most crucial of skills, putting.

Rory Sabbatini plays an approach shot to the green. Sabbatini is one of the PGA Tour's best scramblers. This means completing a hole in par despite not making the Green In Regulation (see page 25).

Tournament Tactics

Consistency and accuracy are essential to win tournaments. Top golfers are aware of their position on the leader board and pick their moments to defend or attack. If they are a shot or two behind the leader with only a few holes to play, they may choose to take a high-risk shot, such as aiming a ball to cross a water hazard at the far end of their hitting range. Alternatively, they may choose to play in their usual way, hoping their opponent makes a mistake. All the time, professional golfers know that one poor swing on the tee or fairway can leave their ball in deep trouble in a lake, rough or trees.

Bouncing Back

Great players are mentally strong. They are good at forgetting a bad shot and focusing on the next one. If they tackle the following shot well, they may have played themselves out of danger. One of the most important skills is for a player to par a hole when he or she is not on the green and has only two shots to make par. This is known as scrambling. It calls for players to execute exceptional pitch and chip shots (see page 26) to get the ball as near to the hole as possible, before making a single putt under pressure. Scrambling is such an important skill that it is one of the statistics recorded on professional tours along with driving distance, accuracy and number of putts taken.

(see page 26)

(see page 32)

Who is...

...Annika Sörenstam?

Annika Sörenstam proved her tactical skill and mental toughness on the way to 88 career wins, including 70 LPGA (see page 32) tournament victories. She began playing golf in her native Sweden at the age of 12 and went on to win ten majors before her retirement in 2008. Awarded the Rolex Player of the Year title eight times, Sörenstam dominated women's golf, becoming the first to shoot a score of 59 at an LPGA tournament in 2001 and winning 11 LPGA tournaments the following year.

STAT ATTACK

Scramble Percentage on the European Tour 2007

Player	% of Scrambles Made
1 Padraig Harrington	63.6
2 Robert Karlsson	62.0
3 Richard Green	61.3
4 Søren Kjeldsen	60.3
5 Niclas Fasth	60.0

Annika Sörenstam plays a shot onto the green at the 2008 Kraft Nabisco Championship, a tournament she won three times.

ON THE TEE

Players play their first shot from the tee. They must play the ball in between, and up to two club lengths behind, the pair of tee markers. In a group, the last player to the hole has the 'honour'. This means that he or she tees off first.

Driving

Players aim to hit a long, accurate drive to put their ball in the best possible position for their next shot. Most golfers use a wood for distance, but if there is a strong wind or the fairway is extremely tight, they may use an iron for extra accuracy instead. With a balanced, wide stance, players concentrate on making a full, smooth swing back and then down and through the ball. Golfers must trust their club to do the work and try not to swing too hard or fast because this tends to result in a bad drive.

STAT ATTACK

Average Driving Distance 2007 LPGA Tour

1	Karin Sjödin	275.8 yards
2	Jee Young Lee	273.1 yards
3	Lorena Ochoa	270.6 yards
4	Brittany Lincicome	270.6 yards
5	Suzann Pettersen	270.3 yards

Ji-Yai Shin of South Korea hits a drive at the 2008 British Open held at the Sunningdale golf course. Just out of her teens, Shin's powerful, accurate driving helped her claim victory.

Who is...

...Sergio Garcia?

Sergio Garcia first picked up a golf club when he was just three years old and is famous for his aggressive, risk-taking play and delicate touch around the greens. He has won 17 tournaments and is a crucial member of Europe's Ryder Cup team. In his debut professional season he duelled with Tiger Woods to finish second at the PGA Championship. He has since finished second again in that tournament and the Open.

The longest male hitters, who can hit a drive over 382.8 yards (350 metres), look to pounce on a shorter-than-average par 4 or par 5 hole. They aim to reach the green in one or two shots, giving themselves a good chance of a birdie. If they cannot reach the green in one shot on a par 4, a long, accurate drive can place players in a perfect position to make a short second shot close to the hole.

STAT ATTACK

Average Driving Distance 2007 PGA Tour

1 Bubba Watson	315.2 yards
2 John Daly	312.9 yards
3 J.B. Holmes	312.6 yards
4 Robert Garrigus	310.5 yards
5 Scott Gutschewski	306.1 yards

Bad Shots, Lost Balls

If a player fails to line up his or her shot well, does not hit the ball cleanly or slices or hooks the ball, it can travel deep into the rough or a hazard. If a player fears his or her ball might be lost or out of bounds, he or she can play a second shot off the tee called a provisional ball. If the first ball is not found within five minutes, the provisional ball becomes the ball in play and the next shot the player takes will be their fourth.

Even if golfers have hit their drive straight and true, if they have worked out their yardage incorrectly or get a bad bounce on the course, the ball can still end up in trouble. Balls can over-run into the rough on the edge of the fairway or come to rest on a tricky fairway slope. Golfers have to adjust their stance and the type of shot they choose, when they play a ball above or below the height of their feet, for example.

Sergio Garcia's fairway shot takes a good-sized divot of grass. Using short irons on the fairway, top players can generate a lot of backspin on the ball.

SHOT SELECTION

Top golfers have an array of shots they can play for different situations. Selecting the best shot for the right situation is the hallmark of champions. Getting it wrong can be an expensive mistake, costing a number of strokes and sometimes, a tournament title.

Playing for Position

Each hole poses different threats to a golfer. Top players will be aware of all the hazards on a hole, and decide before taking a shot where they want to send the ball. They are thinking of the optimum position for their next shot. For example, players may play short of a large bunker or water hazard, a move known as laying up, to give themselves the best position for their next shot. Match situations, however, may force players to gamble on clearing a large fairway bunker or water hazard right at the edge of their range, to try to get a birdie or eagle.

Vijay Singh plays a shot out of some light rough while the crowd look on. Players adjust their swing and choice of club when hitting out of the rough to ensure a clean contact and to get the correct distance on the shot.

Shaping the Ball

Professional golfers look to master skills such as bending the flight of the ball out to the right then curving leftwards, called draw, and the opposite pattern, known as fade.

A top player may hit a ball using draw or fade to counteract a strong wind blowing across the hole. He or she may also use such a technique to send the ball 'round the corner' of an angled dogleg hole to gain extra distance and to get close to the green. Adverse weather conditions, such as gusts of wind, can affect the type of shot played. When facing a strong wind, players sometimes play a low shot so that the wind has less effect on the ball. Other shots are punched low, for example, to avoid low-hanging branches.

Pin Placement

Pin placement is the position of the hole marked by the flag on the green. At competitive tournaments, this usually changes for each round and can cause great debate. Some tournament organisers opt for very aggressive pin placements, for example, close to the edge of a giant slope on the green, or near a bunker or large water hazard. This can mean that players either choose to play the ball safely and aim for the heart of the green away from danger, or they go for it and try to hit the ball really close to the hole. Sometimes, greens have two tiers with a large slope between the two levels. Golfers aim to hit the ball onto the tier containing the hole, because putting up or down giant slopes is notoriously tricky.

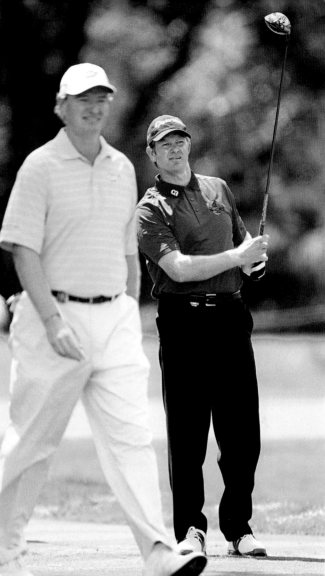

Ernie Els strides away from the tee area after his playing partner, fellow South African, Retief Goosen hits a long accurate drive. Goosen is well-known for his driving accuracy.

STAT ATTACK

Greens In Regulation (GIR)

Recent PGA Tour GIR Leaders

2007 Tiger Woods (71.02%)

2006 Tiger Woods (74.15%)

2005 Sergio Garcia (71.8%)

Recent European Tour GIR Leaders

2007 Retief Goosen (77.0%)

2006 Titch Moore (75.6%)

2005 Ernie Els (76.4%)

SHORT GAME

Shorter shots, usually those hit onto the green, are known as a golfer's short game. Players with an excellent short game can sometimes make up for wayward shots with scintillating pitches, chips and bunker play to save their par on a hole.

Pitches and Chips

The two main short-game shots used are the pitch and the chip. The pitch shot usually requires a lofted club, such as a 9 iron or wedge, which sends the ball up high over an obstacle, such as a water hazard, bushes or bunker. It generates backspin, which helps to stop the ball once it lands. When players generate backspin on their shot, they may aim to hit the ball ahead of the hole and then spin it back towards the hole.

The chip is a low-running shot made with a short swing of a club such as a 6 or 7 iron. The ball travels far lower than a pitch and rolls on when it bounces. Close to the green, the chip is often used to lift the ball up and over the rough so that its first bounce is on the green. From further away, it is used by some players as a lofted putt when there is a clear path to the flag. Like the pitch, the length of a chip shot can be altered by the club used and by the players changing the length of their backswing.

Rocco Mediate plays a short chip shot from just off the green. He aims for the ball to bounce on the green and roll as close as possible, or ideally into, the hole.

STAT ATTACK

Most Birdies Over a 72-Hole PGA Tournament

32 Mark Calcavecchia, 2001 Phoenix Open

32 Paul Gow, 2001 BC Open

31 John Huston, 1998 United Airlines Hawaiian Open

31 Phil Mickelson, 2006 Bell South Classic

Green-side Bunkers

To hit out of a bunker that is beside or relatively close to the green, players need a delicate touch, usually using a sand wedge. The typical shot used is the splash shot, where the player aims the club to hit the sand a short distance (around 3 to 5 centimetres) behind the ball. This sends the ball up and out of the bunker and onto the green. For short splash shots, a golfer opens the club face (the club face is turned to point slightly to the right for a right-handed golfer) to get more height and less distance on the shot.

Phil Mickelson plays an explosive-looking splash shot out of a greenside bunker. A splash shot sees the golfer's club make contact with the sand a few centimetres behind the ball.

Who is...

...Phil Mickelson?

Phil Mickelson is golf's most famous left-handed player and has one of the greatest short games. He has a terrific touch with pitches and chips close to the green and popularised the daring flop shot, where the ball is hit very high over a very short distance. Mickelson's high-risk, aggressive play has won him many fans, 34 PGA tournaments and three Majors but, occasionally, it has also lost him tournaments. He has finished second at the US Open four times.

PRESSURE PUTTING

Tournaments are lost and won on the putting green. Players can drive a ball over 300 yards (274 metres) to reach the green in a single shot, but may take many more to putt the ball into the hole.

MAD //// //// FACT

The longest recorded putt at a Major was a 30-metre-long monster, sunk by Nick Faldo at the Masters in 1989 on his way to victory.

Putting Technique

To putt well, golfers have to be skilled at judging the speed of a shot and the angle or direction required so that the ball rides the slopes and contours of the green and travels towards the hole.

Most golfers use a regular-length putter with a wide stance and their head right over the ball. They keep their head and body still as they take the club back and swing it smoothly through the ball, just skimming the green as they make full contact with the ball. Some golfers prefer using a club with a much longer shaft and grip, known as a broom handle or belly putter. This is swung from the body like a pendulum. Many players, including Vijay Singh and Colin Montgomerie have experimented with these.

K.J. Choi checks the speed of the green with a putt away from the hole during a pre-tournament practise round with Miguel Ángel Jiménez.

Reading the Greens

The player whose ball is furthest from the hole usually takes the first putt. If another player's ball is in any way distracting or in the path of the ball, it is marked by placing a small, flat disc in the ball's place. A good golfer spends some time reading the green, mapping out the curves and slopes of the green and working out in which direction he or she needs to strike the ball to send it curving back towards the hole. Golfers also have to judge the amount of force they need to use to give the ball a chance of reaching the hole but not skating past it. Putts from 2 to 4 metres back to the hole to save par are amongst the most nerve-wracking in golf. When two players have putts from a similar place on the green, the second player to putt usually watches his or her opponent's putt intently for clues about force and direction. This is called 'going to school' on a putt.

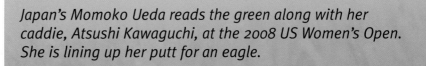

Japan's Momoko Ueda reads the green along with her caddie, Atsushi Kawaguchi, at the 2008 US Women's Open. She is lining up her putt for an eagle.

RECOVERY SHOTS

All golfers encounter difficulties on the course from time to time. What can separate good from great players is how they deal with the ball in tricky lies.

Cause and Effect

Poor shots that direct the ball away from the fairway or green occur for many reasons. Some, such as a sudden gust of wind or bad bounce, are out of a player's control, but most are down to an issue with the player's alignment and swing. A slice, where the ball curves out wide to the right, can occur as a result of a weak grip, the clubface not being lined up behind the ball, or through a poor stance. A hook sees the ball swing out wide towards the left. Both often see the ball land in the rough or trees.

Rough and Trees

The rough and trees that line fairways are designed to penalise poor shots. Golfers use a shorter iron in the rough and aim to hit the ball hard to get it up and out of the grass. Trees can restrict golfers and their club's movement so that they have to use a shortened swing to punch the ball out and back onto the fairway.

The rough away from a fairway can be light, medium or heavy, or in this case, full of cacti. Brett Quigley attempts a shot, turning his clubhead round and playing left-handed to avoid a prickly cactus.

Fairway Bunkers

Golf holes are peppered with bunkers, not just around the green, but along the fairway, too. It is rare for golfers to go a round without finding themselves in the sand. How they play from a bunker is determined by the lie of the ball and the distance from the hole. If the ball is sitting up well in a shallow bunker, players may use a medium iron, such as a 6 iron, or a wood to strike the ball a long distance down the fairway. At the other extreme, a miss-hit shot may see the ball plugged deep into the vertical face of the bunker. In this situation, a golfer may opt to play the ball out sideways rather than risk taking two or three shots in the sand.

Deep Trouble

Sometimes, a golfer may be in serious trouble and he or she will have to hit an unusual shot to get out of difficulty. Many golfers, for example, choose to play their ball out of the shallow water of a stream or pond rather than take a penalty drop. Sometimes, if players cannot get into their normal stance or are unable to make a full swing because the ball is against an obstacle, they may use their putter or turn a long iron round to play the shot backwards. They may even play the shot into a tree to get the ball to rebound off it.

Sometimes, players choose not to add a penalty shot to their score and instead go for a really tough shot playing the ball from where it lies. Here, Nick Faldo, with rolled-up trouser legs, plays out of the water.

THE BIG COMPETITIONS

No one organisation controls all of professional golf and its tournaments. Instead, top professional golfers compete on one of a number of major tours. Each tour holds many tournaments over an almost year-long season.

The PGA Tour and LPGA

The Professional Golfer's Association of America was formed in 1916 and in 1968, a separate organisation, the PGA Tour, was formed. The PGA is the wealthiest tour in the world, with an amazing US$272.3 million prize money paid out during 2007. As a result, it often draws some of the finest golfers from outside North America. The most prestigious tour in women's golf, the LPGA tour began in 1950. Having built upon early successes, the 2008 tour carried prize money totalling more than US$58 million. Although based mainly in the United States, the 2008 tour included tournaments in Japan, China, France, South Africa and three in Mexico, the home nation of one of its leading players, Lorena Ochoa.

The European Tour

The European Tour is an organisation largely controlled by professional golfers who run a tour second only in size and wealth to the PGA Tour. The European Tour consists of around 50 tournaments arranged weekly. In 1989, the Dubai Desert Classic became the first of the tour's tournaments to be held in Asia. Today, the season starts with more than a dozen tournaments in a row in Asia, Australia and the Middle East. The leading money winner over the year wins the coveted Order of Merit title.

Other Tours and Events

Other tours exist, including the Asian Tour, which had 32 events in 2008 and the Japan Golf Tour, which had 25 events in 2008. There are often second-level or satellite tours. The most successful players of these qualify for a place on the main tour. The European Tour, for example, runs a Challenge Tour where any golfer who wins three of its events is allowed to play on the European Tour.

Both the European and PGA Tour run a Senior or Champions Tour for veteran players older than 50. In 2008, amongst the tournament winners were Bernhard Langer, Tom Watson, Scott Hoch and Ian Woosnam. Golfing legend Hale Irwin has won more prize money on the PGA Champions Tour since 1995 (over US$24 million) than he did in his 27 years on the regular PGA Tour.

STAT ATTACK

LPGA Leading Money Winners

2007	Lorena Ochoa
2006	Lorena Ochoa
2005	Annika Sörenstam
2004	Annika Sörenstam
2003	Annika Sörenstam
2002	Annika Sörenstam
2001	Annika Sörenstam
2000	Karrie Webb

Who is...

...Lorena Ochoa?

Ranked as the world's number one female golfer, Lorena Ochoa won her first of 44 amateur events aged six and joined the LPGA Tour in 2003. A remarkably consistent player, Ochoa has won two majors and 21 other LPGA tournaments. In 2007, she recorded 21 top-ten finishes including eight wins and five runner-up spots. Ochoa also led the LPGA Tour in number of birdies made and fewest number of putts.

Lorena Ochoa strikes the ball powerfully during the 2008 US Open. In 2007, Ochoa became the first female golfer to win US$4 million in a season.

THE MASTERS

The four Majors are the most important tournaments and are the career aim for many professional golfers. The first Major of the year is the Masters. It is the only Major that is held at the same course – the Augusta National golf club – every year.

Club and Customs

Four years after retiring from competitive golf, the great Bobby Jones along with Clifford Roberts founded the Augusta National Invitation Tournament at the Augusta National golf club, in Georgia, USA. In 1939, the tournament became known as the Masters. Now held every April, the field at the Masters is smaller than at the other Majors, with players going out in groups of three for the first two rounds. The Masters has a number of other customs. Until 1982, players could not use their own caddies but had to use caddies from the club. The defending Masters champion always plays with the reigning US amateur champion for the first two rounds.

MAD /// /// FACT

The defending champion chooses what the other Masters winners eat at a dinner held in Augusta. Scotsman Sandy Lyle served the champions haggis, whilst Mike Weir chose wild boar.

Trevor Immelman tees off at the Augusta Club in a par 3 contest prior to the 2008 Masters. Immelman became the first South African in 30 years to win the tournament.

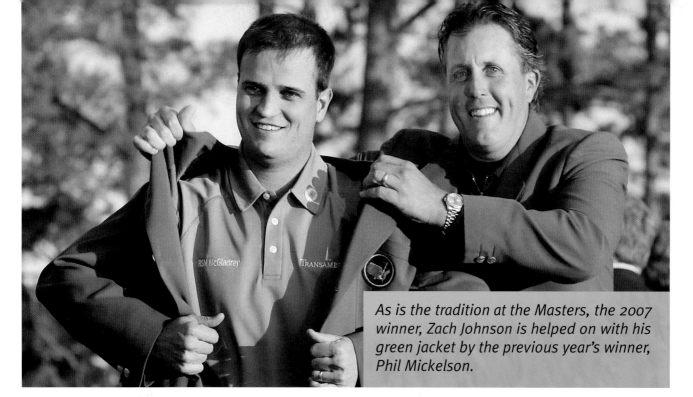

As is the tradition at the Masters, the 2007 winner, Zach Johnson is helped on with his green jacket by the previous year's winner, Phil Mickelson.

The Course

Augusta is famous for its pretty surroundings, which contrast to its brutal holes and deadly greens. Many rounds hinge on how golfers play the tough 11th, 12th and 13th holes, known as Amen Corner. The 11th is the longest par 4 hole on the course, the 13th a challenging par 5, and in between them lies a short 155-yard (141.7-metre) par 3 that players rarely find easy. In the 1980 tournament, Tom Weiskopf took 13 shots to complete this hole! In 1935, the par 5 15th hole saw one of the most famous shots in golf history. Gene Sarazen hit his second shot straight into the hole to record an albatross (3 under par) on the hole and win the tournament.

Masters Winners

The winner of the Masters receives a gold medal, prize money of more than US$1 million and the coveted Green Jacket. In 1997, when he destroyed the field to win by 12 shots, Tiger Woods became the youngest ever winner at 21 years of age. The oldest winner was Jack Nicklaus in 1986 when he was 46.

STAT ATTACK

Recent Masters Winners

2008 - Trevor Immelman

2007 - Zach Johnson

2006 - Phil Mickelson

2005 - Tiger Woods

2004 - Phil Mickelson

2003 - Mike Weir

2002 - Tiger Woods

2001 - Tiger Woods

2000 - Vijay Singh

The Kraft Nabisco Masters

The women's equivalent event is the Kraft Nabisco Masters, which is held at the Mission Hills Country Club in California, USA. Amy Alcott, Dottie Pepper, Betsy King and Annika Sörenstam are all tied on three victories each as the most successful competitors.

THE OPEN CHAMPIONSHIP

The oldest of all of golf's Majors is the Open Championship. In 1860, Prestwick Golf Club in Scotland was the location for its first contest between just eight players.

Qualifying and Prize Money

A total of 156 golfers start each Open. About two-thirds of these do not have to qualify for the tournament because they are leading players on the various tours. Others qualify through tournaments or in international qualifying competitions. Once in the Open, the aim is to survive the cut after two rounds and strive to be on the leader board. The first prize money awarded was in 1863; just £10, which had to be split between the second, third and fourth placed players, with the winner receiving a belt! The 2008 competition featured a total prize money of £4.2 million with the winner receiving £750,000.

MAD FACT

At the 2000 Open, Tiger Woods finished at 19 under par, an Open record. He never sent the ball into a bunker on any of the 72 holes.

Courses

The Open is held on different courses rotating between England and Scotland. Since 1922, the tournament has always been held on a links course. These courses are often near the coast. They have few trees and water hazards, but thick rough up and down the fairway and strong, unpredictable winds. They are considered stern tests of a golfer's skill.

St Andrews has held the Open 27 times and will host the tournament in 2010, while Turnberry in Scotland hosted the 2009 competition. The Open has also been held at Carnoustie, Royal Troon, Royal Birkdale and Muirfield. Unlike the other Majors, the Open features an exciting four-hole play-off system if any leaders are tied on the same number of shots after 72 holes. This was used in 2007 to separate Padraig Harrington from Sergio Garcia after a thrilling contest.

STAT ATTACK

Recent Open Winners

2008	Padraig Harrington
2007	Padraig Harrington
2006	Tiger Woods
2005	Tiger Woods
2004	Todd Hamilton
2003	Ben Curtis
2002	Ernie Els
2001	David Duval
2000	Tiger Woods

Who is...

...Padraig Harrington?

Padraig Harrington entered his fifth Ryder Cup in 2008 as Europe's best golfer. He joined the European Tour in 1996 and has shown great accuracy and consistency to finish in the top ten of the European Order of Merit seven times. In 2007, he became the first golfer from the Republic of Ireland to win the Open after a nail-biting final round and four hole play-off against Sergio Garcia. He repeated his Open win in 2008, winning by four shots. In 2008, he also won his third major, with two superb rounds of 66 to win the PGA Championship.

Open Winners

Amateur golfers are admitted into the Open with the leading amateur winning a medal and, in modern times, often using it as a springboard to a professional career. This was the case with Justin Rose who was an amateur when he finished fourth in 1998 and Chris Wood who tied for fifth place in the 2008 Open and turned professional weeks afterwards. There have been only six amateur winners of the tournament since 1928. Amongst the professionals, players such as Harry Vardon with six titles and Tom Watson with five stand out. Of the winners of the Open so far, 26 have been American, 22 Scottish, 14 English and four Australian. Ireland is seventh on the list purely due to the efforts of Padraig Harrington who won back to back victories in 2007 and 2008.

STAT ATTACK

Recent Women's Open Winners

Year	Winner
2008	Ji-Yai Shin
2007	Lorena Ochoa
2006	Sherri Steinhauer
2005	Jeong Jang
2004	Karen Stupples
2003	Annika Sörenstam
2002	Karrie Webb
2001	Se Ri Pak
2000	Sophie Gustafson

Padraig Harrington lines up a crucial putt at the 2008 Open. Despite missing out on practise before the tournament with a wrist injury, he was triumphant, winning his second Open in a row.

THE US OPEN AND PGA CHAMPIONSHIPS

The US Open and PGA Championships are both held on different courses in the United States. The US Open is traditionally the second Major of the year and the PGA, held in August, the last.

The US Open

The first US Open was held in 1895 on a nine-hole course at Newport, Rhode Island. A number of players qualify to join former winners and the top-ranked players in the competition. The youngest ever qualifier was Tadd Fujikawa in 2006. He was just 15. From 1926 to 2000, the only non-Americans to win the US Open were South Africa's Gary Player (1965) and Ernie Els (1994 and 1997), England's Tony Jacklin (1970) and Australia's David Graham (1981). Since then, the competition winners have come from South Africa, Australia, New Zealand and Argentina. In 2007, Ángel Cabrera became only the second Argentinean to win a Major with a one stroke victory over Jim Furyk and Tiger Woods. The following year saw a stunning performance from Tiger Woods who struggled with a knee injury throughout the tournament, but holed an amazing birdie putt on the last hole to go into an 18 hole play-off against Rocco Mediate, which Woods won.

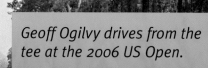

Geoff Ogilvy drives from the tee at the 2006 US Open.

STAT ATTACK

Recent US Open Winners

2008 Tiger Woods

2007 Ángel Cabrera

2006 Geoff Ogilvy

2005 Michael Campbell

2004 Retief Goosen

2003 Jim Furyk

2002 Tiger Woods

2001 Retief Goosen

2000 Tiger Woods

The PGA Championship

The PGA Championship began in 1916. In 1958 the format of the tournament turned from match play to stroke play (see page 11). Today, over 100,000 spectators flock to the competition to watch players compete for the Wanamaker Trophy. The tournament has seen some surprising winners but none more so than John Daly who was ninth reserve for the 1991 tournament. With no time to play a practise round, Daly went out using another player's caddie and won by three shots.

Ángel Cabrera looks unimpressed with his putt at the 2007 US Open, but he shot a final round of 69 to win the tournament by one stroke from Jim Furyk and Tiger Woods.

The LPGA Championship and US Open

The calendar for women's Majors is a little different from the men's, with the LPGA Championship second, the US Open third and the British Open last in the season. The LPGA began in 1955 with prize money of US$6,000. In 2008, that figure was US$2 million with US$300,000 going to the winner, Yani Tseng from Taiwan, who at 19 years of age, was the tournament's youngest ever winner. In quite a coincidence, the winner of the 2008 Women's US Open was also just 19 and from Asia – Inbee Park from South Korea.

THE RYDER AND SOLHEIM CUPS

Professional golfers are individual sportsmen but in a small number of competitions, they compete as a pair or team. The most famous of all team golf competitions is the Ryder Cup. The women's equivalent is the Solheim Cup.

The Ryder Cup

The Ryder Cup is a team match play golf competition. Held over three days, each team strives to win 14 points to secure the trophy. In the event of a 14–14 tie, the cup holders retain the trophy. The first two days are taken up with eight matches, featuring pairs from each team trying to win their match and to secure a point for their side. The last day sees all 12 players on each team play a match against an individual opponent.

Originally played between the US and Great Britain, the US were so dominant that Great Britain won only once and drew once between 1933 and 1979. In 1979, the British team included European players, too. Buoyed by players of the calibre of Seve Ballesteros, Europe fought back, winning its first competition in 1985 as well as the first three Ryder Cups of the twenty-first century before the US victory in 2008.

Luke Donald lines up a putt with the help of his playing partner, Sergio Garcia at the 2006 Ryder Cup.

S T A T A T T A C K

Rencet Ryder Cup Winners

2008	USA 16½ - Europe 11½
2006	Europe 18 - USA 9
2004	Europe 18 - USA 9
2002	Europe 15 - USA 12
1999	USA 14 - Europe 13
1997	Europe 14 - USA 13
1995	Europe 14 - USA 13
1993	USA 15 - Europe 13
1991	USA 14 - Europe 13
1989	Europe 14 - USA 14

Team Selection

Professional golfers work hard to make the 12-player team. The European team picks ten golfers based on ranking points secured on the European Tour and the World Ranking points list. The American team picks eight of its players based on money won from events. The team captains fill the rest of their team with wild card picks. At the tournament, the captain cajoles his players to produce their best and has to choose pairings for the first two days' matches trying to ensure good chemistry between the players.

The Solheim Cup

The Solheim Cup began in 1990. Teams of 12 American and European golfers compete against each other. Since 2002, the Solheim has mimicked the Ryder Cup in featuring 28 matches for the trophy. The Americans have been more successful with seven victories, while Laura Davies holds an incredible record of competing in all the Solheim Cups held so far.

Solheim Cup Winners

2007 USA 16 - Europe 12

2005 USA 15 - Europe 12

2003 Europe 17 - USA 10

2002 USA 15 - Europe 12

2000 Europe 14 - USA 11

1998 USA 16 - Europe 12

1996 USA 17 - Europe 11

1994 USA 13 - Europe 7

1992 Europe 11 - USA 6

1990 USA 11 - Europe 4

Suzann Pettersen drops to her knees as she misses a putt during her singles match in the 2007 Solheim Cup. A former LPGA Championship winner, Pettersen lost this match to Stacy Prammanasudh.

GOLFING LEGENDS

Over the years, the game of golf has been graced by some incredible players. Here are six of the very best who have left their mark on the sport.

Jack Nicklaus

The 'Golden Bear' is considered the greatest professional golfer of all time, a title that only Tiger Woods may take from him in the future. Hugely strong mentally and physically, Nicklaus won a staggering 18 Majors. He finished second in 19 further Majors and was the leading money winner eight times. He won more than 100 tournaments worldwide and holds the record for winning six Masters.

Gary Player

Supremely fit, practising and training incredibly hard, Player became one of the 'big three' along with Palmer and Nicklaus who helped popularise golf. He won nine Majors with his last, the 1978 US Masters at the age of 42. In total, the 'Dark Knight' won an incredible 163 tournaments worldwide travelling over 22 million kilometres in the process.

Arnold Palmer

Turning professional after winning the 1954 US Amateur Championship, Arnold Palmer revitalised US interest in the sport with his attacking play. His charisma, charm and aggressive style endeared him to the public. He won over 60 PGA Tour events in the 1960s and early 1970s and in 1963 became the first player to win US$100,000 in a season. In 2004, he made his 50th and last consecutive appearance at the US Masters, the Major that he won four times.

Four of the golf's greatest players (Gary Player, Jack Nicklaus, Arnold Palmer and Tom Watson) pose for a photograph during a casual match in California, USA in 1983.

Tom Watson

Born in Kansas City, USA, Watson turned professional in 1971 and won his first of eight majors four years later. Not the longest driver, but consistent, Watson was considered the best bad weather player in the world and triumphed frequently on the toughest courses and in the worst conditions. Amongst his many memorable performances were many epic battles with Jack Nicklaus. Watson was the first player to win US$500,000 in a year and was the world number one ranked played from 1978 to 1982.

S T A T A T T A C K

Most Major Championships Won by Male Golfers

Jack Nicklaus - 18

Tiger Woods - 13

Walter Hagen - 11

Ben Hogan - 9

Gary Player - 9

Tom Watson - 8

Bobby Jones - 7

Arnold Palmer - 7

Gene Sarazen - 7

Sam Snead - 7

Harry Vardon - 7

Severiano Ballesteros

One of the most-loved of all European golfers, Seve Ballesteros was the ultimate in swashbuckling players. Frequently inaccurate off the tee, the Spaniard's short game verged on genius as he coaxed high-risk winning shots from between trees, deep bunkers and even from car parks. He announced his brilliance at the age of 19 with second place in the 1976 Open and went on to win five Majors and 94 tournaments in total. He will be most fondly remembered for revitalising the Ryder Cup when his passion saw him play or captain four winning European sides.

Seve Ballesteros helps Tom Watson with the famous green jacket of a Masters winner in 1981.

GLOSSARY

Albatross Completing a hole in three shots under par by holing your second shot on a par 5 or having a hole in one on a par 4 hole.

Approach A shot hit aiming for the green.

Birdie Finishing a hole one shot under par.

Bogey Finishing a hole one shot over par.

Bunker A depression on the course filled with sand, which must be raked after a shot is taken.

Caddie A person who carries a player's bag of clubs an offers advice on the yardage of each hole.

Carry The distance the ball flies through the air without bouncing.

Chip A short stabbed shot normally onto the green.

Divot A piece of turf torn out of the ground by a shot.

Dogleg A hole that is angled or curved from left to right or from right to left.

Draw A shot where, for a right-handed player, the ball starts right then curves through the air to the left.

Eagle Finishing a hole in two shots under par.

Etiquette Good behaviour and consideration for other golfers and the course.

Fade A shot where, for a right-handed player, the ball starts left then curves through the air from left to right.

Fairway The cut grass between the tee and the green.

Green In Regulation Getting the ball on to the green in the hole's par score minus two shots.

Handicap A system used in amateur golf to give players of different abilities a chance to play against each other on an equal footing.

Hazards Features of a golf course such as bunkers, ditches, a stream or lake which make the course more challenging.

Loft   The amount of angle on the club face, which determines how high in the air the ball will carry. A pitching wedge, for example, has much more loft than a 3 iron.

Par   The number of shots the officials of a golf club feel that a hole should be completed in by a skilled player.

Pin Position   The location of the hole on the green. At tournaments, this is often changed between rounds.

Professional   To be paid to play golf either through appearance fees, winning prize money at tournaments or being sponsored by companies.

Putt   A shot usually made on the green or close to it, where the ball is rolled along the ground using a putter.

Round   The word used for playing all the holes in a golf course.

Tee   The rectangular area at the start of a golf hole where players make their first shot, their drive, from.

Tee   A small plastic or wooden peg that raises the ball off the ground and is used only on the tee for the first shot of each hole.

Yardage   The distance from the tee to the flag on a golf course. Top players or their caddies carry charts showing detailed distances of all the major points on a golf hole.

WEBSITES

WWW.GOLF-FOUNDATION.ORG

A useful website introducing golf to beginners and young players which includes playing tips and guides to rules and getting started.

WWW.LPGA.COM

The official website of the LPGA tour which contains facts and video footage of the top female golfers and news of upcoming tournaments on the tour.

WWW.WGV.COM/HOF/HOF.PHP

The World Golf Hall of Fame contains detailed and interesting profiles on 120 of world golf's greatest male and female players.

WWW.PGATOUR.COM

The website of the US PGA Tour is packed full of details of forthcoming and previous tournaments, player profiles and lots of videos on PGA players and courses.

WWW.EUROPEANTOUR.COM

The official website of the PGA European Tour. This website has news, photos, videos and features from tour events and Ryder Cups.

INDEX

albatross 10, 35, 44
amateur 37, 42

backspin 23, 26
bag 9, 14, 15, 18, 20, 22
ball 6, 8, 9, 10, 12, 14, 15, 16, 21, 22, 23, 24, 25, 26, 27, 28, 29, 30, 31
Ballesteros, Severiano 40, 43
birdie 10, 23, 24, 33, 38, 44
bogey 10, 44
bunker 6, 7, 10, 13, 14, 17, 20, 24, 25, 26, 27, 31, 43, 44

Cabrera, Angel 38
caddie 18, 19, 29, 34, 39, 44
chip 20, 21, 26, 27, 44
clothing 15
club (association) 34
club (equipment) 6, 8, 9, 10, 11, 14, 15, 17, 18, 19, 20, 22, 23, 24, 26, 27, 28, 30, 31
    broom handle 28
    iron 11, 14, 15, 22, 23, 26, 30, 31
    putter 14, 28, 31
    wedge 14, 26, 27
    wood 14, 22, 31
coach 18, 19
competition (see tournament)
course 6, 8, 9, 12, 13, 17, 19, 23, 30, 34, 35, 36, 38, 43
cut 7, 36

Daly, John 39
Davies, Laura 41
divot 13, 23, 44
double-bogey 10
draw 25, 44
drive 6, 14, 15, 20, 22, 23, 25, 28, 43
driving range 12, 19
Duval, David 11, 16, 36

eagle 10, 24, 29, 44
Edinburgh 8, 9
Els, Ernie 7, 19, 25, 32, 36, 38
equipment 9, 14–15
etiquette 9, 44
Europe 8, 23, 32, 34, 37, 40, 41

fade 25, 44
fairway 6, 12, 13, 14, 20, 21, 22, 23, 24, 30, 31, 36, 44
Faldo, Nick 18, 19, 28, 31
flag 6, 16, 19, 25, 26
Fujikawa, Tadd 38
Furyk, Jim 38, 39

Garcia, Sergio 7, 9, 16, 18, 23, 25, 36, 40
Goosen, Retief 25, 32, 38
grass 6, 12, 13, 23, 30
green 6, 9, 10, 12, 13, 14, 15, 17, 19, 20, 23, 25, 26, 27, 28, 29, 30, 31, 35

handicap 11, 44
Harman, Butch 19
Harrington, Padraig 7, 17, 21, 32, 36, 37, 39
hazard 13, 14, 19, 21, 23, 24, 25, 26, 36, 44
history 8–9
hole 6, 7, 9, 10, 11, 13, 16, 17, 18, 19, 20, 21, 22, 23, 24, 25, 26, 28, 29, 31, 35, 38
hole-in-one 7, 10

Immelman, Trevor 19, 35
Irwin, Hale 33

Japan 16, 32, 33
Johnson, Zach 35
Jones, Bobby 34, 43

Langer, Bernhard 33
Leadbetter, David 19
lie 16, 30, 31
loft 14, 26, 45

McLean, Elsie 10
Mediate, Rocco 26, 38
Mickelson, Phil 7, 26, 27, 35, 39
money 18, 32, 33, 35, 36, 39, 41, 42, 43
Montgomerie, Colin 28, 32

Nicklaus, Jack 35, 42, 43
Norman, Greg 19

Ochoa, Lorena 22, 32, 33, 37
officials 17
Ogilvy, Geoff 38

Palmer, Arnold 42, 43
par 10, 11, 13, 20, 21, 23, 26, 29, 35, 45
penalty shot 16, 17, 18, 31
Pettersen, Suzann 22, 41
pin placement 25, 45
pitch 9, 21, 26, 27
Player, Gary 15, 38, 42, 43
play-off 7, 36
Poulter, Ian 15
practise 11, 12, 19, 20, 37
professional 6, 11, 15, 18, 20, 21, 25, 32, 34, 37, 40, 41, 42, 43, 45
Professional Golf Association (PGA) 7, 27, 32
putt 9, 11, 12, 17, 20, 21, 25, 26, 28–29, 33, 37, 38, 39, 41, 45

rankings 7, 43
Roberts, Clifford 34
rough 6, 13, 16, 20, 21, 23, 24, 26, 30, 36
round 6, 7, 11, 19, 25, 34, 35, 36, 45
rules 8, 15, 16–17

sand 6, 12, 17, 27, 31
Sarazen, Gene 35, 43
score 10, 11, 16, 17

Scotland 8, 9, 36
scrambling 20, 21
Shin, Ji-Yai 22, 37
shot 7, 9, 10, 11, 13, 14, 16, 17, 19, 20, 21, 22, 23, 24, 25, 26, 27, 28, 30, 35, 39
Singh, Vijay 7, 24, 28, 32, 35, 39
slope 6, 23, 25, 28, 29
Sörenstam, Annika 21, 33, 35, 37
sponsorship 15, 18
stance 10, 22, 23, 28, 30, 31
Stenson, Henrik 18
St Andrews 8, 9, 36
Sunesson, Fanny 18
swing 10, 19, 21, 22, 24, 26, 28, 30, 31

tactics 20–21, 24, 25, 29
technique 6, 10, 20–21, 25, 28, 29
tee (area) 6, 10, 13, 14, 15, 16, 19, 21, 22, 23, 25, 45
tee (peg) 15
tree 13, 16, 21, 30, 31, 36, 43
tours 32, 33, 34, 36, 37, 42
    Asian Tour 33
    European Tour 32, 34, 37
    Japan Golf Tour 33
    LPGA Tour 32, 33
    PGA Tour 32, 33, 42
tournaments 6, 7, 8, 11, 12, 13, 14, 15, 16, 17, 18, 19, 20, 21, 22, 23, 24, 25, 27, 28, 29, 32, 33, 34, 35, 36, 37, 38, 39, 40, 41, 42, 43
    Kraft Nabisco Championship 21, 35
    LPGA Championship 39, 41
    Majors 27, 28, 33, 34, 35, 36, 37, 38, 39, 42, 43
    The Masters 11, 18, 28, 34–35, 42
    The Open Championship 8, 18, 22, 36–37, 39
    The PGA Championship 13, 16, 23, 37, 38, 39
    The Ryder Cup 11, 23, 37, 40–41, 43
    The Solheim Cup 40–41
    The US Open 7, 27, 29, 33, 38, 39

United States 8, 12, 13, 32, 38, 40, 41

Varden, Harry 37, 43

water feature 6, 13, 21, 24, 25, 26, 31, 36
Watson, Tom 33, 37, 42, 43
weather 22, 25, 30, 36, 43
Weir, Mike 17, 35
Weiskopf, Tom 35
Wie, Michelle 18, 19
Williams, Steve 18
Wilson, Dean 9
Wood, Chris 37
Woods, Tiger 7, 18, 19, 23, 25, 32, 35, 36, 38, 39, 42, 43
Woosnam, Ian 18, 33

yardage 19, 23, 45